THE CUMBRIA
COLOURING BOOK

T0346750

First published 2017
Reprinted 2017, 2018, 2019, 2023, 2024

The History Press
97 St George's Place,
Cheltenham, GL50 3QB
www.thehistorypress.co.uk

Text © The History Press, 2017
Illustrations by Sally Townsend © The History Press, 2017

The right of The History Press to be identified as the Author
of this work has been asserted in accordance with the
Copyright, Designs and Patents Act 1988.

All rights reserved. No part of this book may be reprinted
or reproduced or utilised in any form or by any electronic,
mechanical or other means, now known or hereafter invented,
including photocopying and recording, or in any information storage or retrieval
system, without the permission in writing from the Publishers.

British Library Cataloguing in Publication Data.
A catalogue record for this book is available from the British Library.

ISBN 978 0 7509 7998 6

Typesetting and origination by The History Press
Printed and bound in Turkey by Imak.

THE CUMBRIA
COLOURING BOOK

PAST AND PRESENT

Take some time out of your busy life to relax and unwind with this feel-good colouring book designed for everyone who loves Cumbria.

Absorb yourself in the simple action of colouring in the scenes and settings from around the county, past and present. From majestic mountains and picturesque lakes to historic street scenes, you are sure to find some of your favourite locations waiting to be transformed with a splash of colour.

There are no rules – choose any page and any choice of colouring pens or pencils you like to create your own unique, colourful and creative illustrations.

A shepherd and his dog herd a flock
of sheep on the shoulders of Skiddaw ▸

Allan Bank, once home to William Wordsworth, Grasmere ▸

The Dock Museum, Barrow-in-Furness ▸

Bowness-on-Windermere ▶

A delivery van belonging to Jarman & Sons of the Belvedere
Street Dairy, Workington, at the turn of the century ▸

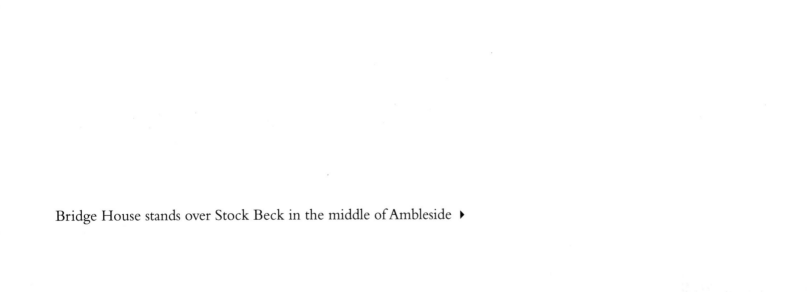

Bridge House stands over Stock Beck in the middle of Ambleside ▸

Buttermere Lake ▸

Carlisle Castle ▸

Carlisle Cathedral ▸

A fine view is on offer from
the top of Cat Bells fell ▶

Cockermouth ▶

Cockermouth, *c.* 1980, with brewery buildings on the left
and what was originally Wharton's linen mill on the right ▸

Cumbrian sheep ▸

Derwent Water ▶

Donkey rides on Seascale beach
in the late nineteenth century ▸

Dove Cottage, Grasmere, where William
Wordsworth wrote some of his greatest poetry ▸

Fisher Street, Carlisle, *c.* 1970 ▸

Fleming Square, Maryport ▶

Furness Railway steam locomotive ▸

Kendal in the 1930s ▸

Kirby Lonsdale Market Square
at the turn of the century ▶

Passengers enjoy a trip across Lake
Windermere aboard *Miss Lakeland II* ▸

Maryport harbour in
the early twentieth century ▸

An MG TF 1250 on display at the
Lakeland Motor Museum, Ulverston ▸

Motoring along Ullswater in the 1920s ▶

Steam train on the Ravenglass
and Eskdale Railway ▸

Cumbria is home to a great variety of wildlife, including
Red Squirrels, Golden Eagles, Ospreys and Red Deer ▸

The River Kent, Kendal ▸

Rydal Water ▶

Scafell Pike is the highest mountain in England ▶

Keswick at the turn of the century ▸

Seascale beach ▶

Slater Bridge, Little Langdale ▸

Wray Castle, Ambleside ▸

The National Trust's steam yacht *Gondola* is a
Victorian steam-powered yacht on Coniston Water ▸

The Square, Ulverston, *c.* 1870 ▶

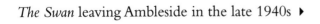

The Swan leaving Ambleside in the late 1940s ▸

The van of the Cumberland Pencil Co. Ltd
at Cumberland Pencil Museum, Keswick ▸

The World of Beatrix Potter, Bowness-on-Windermere ▶

The Lakeside and Haverthwaite Railway ▸

Tullie House Museum & Art Gallery, Carlisle ▸

Whitehaven ▸

Honister Pass in the Lake District ▸

Furness Abbey ▶

The Beacon Museum, Whitehaven ▸

Also from The History Press

Find this colouring book and more at

www.thehistorypress.co.uk